SHEET PAN COOKING COOKBOOK

Your Handy Booklet to Make Delicious, Fast, Affordable, and Quick Weight Loss Meals with Sheet Pan in 30 Minutes or Less – A Gift for Beginners

Table of Contents

INTRODUCTION

A sheet pan takes the idea of a one-pot feast and flips it onto a pan. It saves time, makes tidy up simpler, and doesn't need costly hardware or extravagant ingredients. Simply start with your protein of decision, at that point add vegetables, fat and flavorings, and dish at high heat until everything is brilliant brown.

You can reheat meat, chicken, or nearly anything in a pan on the oven. The key is to keep heat low to abstain from overcooking. Prior to putting meat in the pan, add a touch of oil or your decision of spread. For more dampness, cover the pan while the meat reheats.

Tidying up

This is the part everybody detests, and as it should be. It's difficult to fit a sheet pan into the sink, and definitely water sprinkles all over the place. Here's the way to make the tidy up less hopeless.

1. Prior to setting up the supper, use aluminum foil or material paper so the food will not contact the sheet pan. It will make for a lot quicker cleanup.

2. Utilize a cover when washing the dishes. In any event, don't wear your number one shirt in the kitchen.

3. Use brillo cushions.

4. Pour some bubbling water and a touch of dish cleanser onto the pan and stand by a couple of moments. Really at that time begin cleaning.

5. On the off chance that the scouring gets excessively hard, utilize a degreaser like Easy-Off - simply splash it on the pan, stand by a couple of moments at that point wash off. At that point utilize ordinary dish cleanser and a wipe.

1. Sheet Pan Steak Fajitas

Planning Time: 13 mins | Cook Time: 15 mins |
Complete Time: 33 mins

Fixings
Flavors:

- 2 teaspoons stew powder
- 1 teaspoon cumin
- 1 teaspoon garlic powder
- 1 teaspoons smoked paprika
- 1/2 - 1 teaspoon ocean salt or to taste
- 1/8 teaspoon cayenne pepper discretionary or to taste
- For the Fajitas:
- 12 ounces flank steak cut into 1/4" strips across the grain
- 3 Tablespoons olive oil isolated
- 1 1/2 Tablespoons new cilantro finely slashed
- juice from 2 limes isolated
- 1/2 teaspoon Worcestershire sauce
- 4 medium ringer peppers meagerly cut (I utilized red, yellow, orange and green)
- 1 medium red onion meagerly cut

- For Serving:
- chopped new cilantro
- lime wedges
- sliced avocado
- your most loved natively constructed paleo/Whole30 or locally acquired consistent tortillas
- FOR LOW CARB: low carb tortillas or cauliflower rice, for serving
- FOR MEAL PREP: Lunch compartments

Guidelines
1. Preheat stove to 400 degrees and oil a huge heating sheet (mine was 18 x 13 - utilize two if fundamental).
2. For simpler cleanup, you can likewise fix with material paper or foil.
3. Combine the elements for the flavors in little bowl or sack and blend.
4. In a huge zip-top pack, add the steak and shower with 1/2 tablespoons olive oil, juice from 1 lime, Worcestershire sauce and slashed cilantro. Sprinkle with 2/3 of the fajita flavors. Throw to cover well. (On the off chance that time licenses, permit to marinate in any event 30 minutes or canvassed in the refrigerator for as long as 3 hours for greatest flavor).
5. Spread the vegetables in an even layer on arranged sheet dish. Do whatever it takes not to cover excessively and keep everything in a solitary layer. (Utilize two sheet containers if important). Sprinkle with staying 1/2 tablespoons olive oil and season with staying 33% (1/3) of the flavors. Throw to cover well.

6. Bake in preheated broiler for 10-15 minutes (contingent upon how done you like your vegetables) or until peppers are delicate. (On the off chance that steak was marinating in the cooler, eliminate and permit to sit at room temperature while the vegetables are cooking).
7. Remove sheet skillet from broiler, flip and push the vegetables to the sides of the dish. Add steak strips in a solitary layer to the focal point of the skillet, trying not to pack the dish. Cook on high for 3 minutes or until wanted doneness (flip on a case by case basis).
8. Serve with your most loved natively constructed or locally acquired paleo/low carb/Whole30 tortillas with cut avocado and your #1 fixings.
9. To prepare tortillas: enclose by aluminum foil and add to the top rack of the stove while the chicken is heating for around 5 minutes.

2. Hotdog and Root Vegetable Scramble

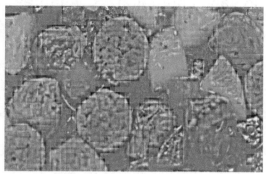

Planning Time: 15 minutes | Cook Time: 20 minutes | Complete Time: 35 minutes | Servings: 4 servings

Fixings

- 2 tbsp. olive oil, isolated
- 4 turkey wieners
- 1 little yam, cleaved
- 1 cup Brussels sprouts, cut fifty-fifty
- 2 medium-sized beets, hacked
- 1 red pepper, hacked
- 2 cloves garlic, minced
- 1 tsp. rosemary
- 1/2 tsp. salt
- 1/2 tsp. pepper

Directions

1. Preheat broiler to 450 F. Warmth 1 tbsp. olive oil over medium warmth in an enormous skillet. Add turkey wieners and cook for 7-8 minutes until seared however not exactly cooked in the center.
2. Meanwhile, add veggies to an enormous heating sheet and throw with olive oil, garlic,

rosemary, salt and pepper. Prepare in the stove for 15 minutes until veggies are delicate.

3. Remove from broiler and add turkey wiener, cooking an additional 5 minutes. Eliminate from stove, serve and appreciate!

3. Sheet Pan Beef and Broccoli

Yield: 4 | planning time 5 minutes | cook time 10 minutes | all out time 15 minutes

Fixings

- 1/2 cup low-sodium soy sauce
- 4 to 5 cloves garlic, finely minced or squeezed
- 2 to 3 tablespoons nectar
- 2 tablespoons earthy colored sugar, pressed
- 2 tablespoons sesame oil
- 2 tablespoons rice vinegar
- 2 to 3 teaspoons ground ginger
- 1 teaspoon genuine salt, discretionary and to taste (soy sauce as of now has salt)
- 1 teaspoon newly ground dark pepper, or to taste
- squeeze cayenne pepper or red pepper chips, discretionary and to taste
- 1 to 1.25 pounds flank steak, cut contrary to what would be expected in scaled down pieces
- around 4 to 6 cups broccoli florets
- 1 tablespoon cornstarch, discretionary
- 1 tablespoon cold water, discretionary

- 2 to 3 green onions cut in 1-inch portions on the inclination, discretionary for embellishing
- 1 tablespoon sesame seeds, discretionary for decorating

Guidelines

1. Preheat broiler to 425F and fix a sheet skillet with aluminum foil for simpler cleanup; put away.
2. To a huge bowl add the soy sauce, garlic, nectar, earthy colored sugar, sesame oil, rice vinegar, ginger, discretionary salt, pepper, discretionary cayenne or red pepper drops, and race to join.
3. Add the steak, mix to consolidate, and allow it to marinate for 10 to 15 minutes (on the off chance that you have time and can marinate for as long as 60 minutes, far better).
4. Using an utensils or an opened spoon, move the steak to the sheet container with space in the middle of the pieces; put away.
5. Add the broccoli (I utilize 6 cups since we like a great deal of broccoli, utilize less whenever wanted) to the marinade blend and give it a fast dunk, you simply need to dampen it a piece.
6. Using an utensils or an opened spoon, move the broccoli to the sheet container, and dissipate it in the middle of the steak if conceivable so food isn't covering excessively; hold the marinade.
7. Bake for around 10 to 12 minutes or until the steak are cooked through and the broccoli is fork-delicate.

8. While the food prepares, alternatively add the held marinade to a little pan and heat it to the point of boiling over medium-high warmth.
9. Add the cornstarch and cold water to a little bowl, mix to join, and all the cornstarch slurry to the bubbling pot, whisking almost continually for 30 seconds or until disintegrated.
10. The sauce will get thick rapidly on the grounds that there's very little amount. Whenever wanted, add around 1/4 to 1/2 cup water as wanted for consistency, racing until joined and smooth.
11. After the hamburger and broccoli are done, equally sprinkle with the sauce, to taste.
12. Evenly embellishment with discretionary green onions, discretionary sesame seeds, and serves right away.

4. Sheet Pan Asian Salmon and Broccoli

Planning time 5 minutes | cook time 15 minutes| complete time 20 minutes | yield: 4

Fixings

- 1.50 pound skin-on salmon filet
- 3 cups broccoli florets
- 3 to 4 tablespoons nectar
- 3 tablespoons decreased sodium light soy sauce (utilize affirmed GF if this is critical to you)
- 3 tablespoons sesame oil
- 1 stacking tablespoon bean stew garlic sauce, or diminished to taste for less warmth
- 1 tablespoon rice vinegar (another vinegar might be subbed)
- Optional new cilantro, for decorating

Guidelines

1. Preheat broiler to 375F (use convection on the off chance that you have it), line a preparing sheet with aluminum foil for simpler cleanup (enthusiastically suggested), shower with cooking splash, place the salmon skin-side down on the heating sheet, and settle the broccoli straight around it, uniformly separated; put away.

2. To a little bowl, add every excess fixing (aside from cilantro), and gradually spoons the majority of the blend over the salmon, and simply dab the broccoli with the sauce.

3. It will retain the overflow sauce from the salmon so no compelling reason to put a lot of sauce on it from the start.

4. Bake for 375F for around 12 to 15 minutes, or until salmon is almost done. Go Broiler to High, and sear for 3 to 5 minutes to complete the process of cooking.

5. Note - Keep a vigilant gaze on your food in the event that you cook it on the grounds that the nectar in the sauce will be inclined to consuming and it can go from fine hoping to consumed in under 1 moment so don't leave the kitchen and watch it the entire time.

6. Alternatively, in case you're not happy with cooking, essentially keep preparing the salmon for a couple of additional minutes, or until done; don't overcook or the salmon will be dry and the broccoli will consume.

Tip - Read blog entry for ideas about how to know when salmon is finished.

7. All pieces differ in their thickness and hence all cooking times will shift. You should be the adjudicator of when it's set and not pass by exclusively what the clock says.

8. Optionally topping with cilantro and serve right away. Formula is best new yet will save hermetically sealed in the ice chest for as long as 4 days.

5. Sheet Pan Salt and Vinegar Chicken and Broccoli

Planning time 5 minutes | Cook time 15 minutes | Complete time 20 minutes | Yield: 5

Fixings

- 1.75 to 2 pounds boneless skinless chicken bosom, diced into scaled down pieces
- 4 cups broccoli florets, diced into enormous ish scaled down pieces
- 6 tablespoons olive oil, separated
- genuine salt and newly ground dark pepper, to taste
- 3 tablespoons apple juice vinegar
- 1 stacking teaspoon dried dill
- 3/4 teaspoon garlic powder
- 1/2 teaspoon granulated sugar, discretionary and to taste
- newly ground Parmesan cheddar, discretionary for decorating

Guidelines

1. Preheat broiler to 475F (use convection in the event that you have it), line a half-sheet container with aluminum foil for simpler cleanup whenever wanted, add the chicken, broccoli (see Note 1 underneath about truly fresh broccoli), uniformly sprinkle with 3 tablespoons olive oil, and season liberally with salt and pepper, and throw with your hands to equitably cover, and meal for 8 minutes.
2. While chicken and broccoli cooks, to a little bowl, add the excess 3 tablespoons olive oil, apple juice vinegar, dill, garlic, discretionary sugar, and mix to consolidate.
3. After 8 minutes, eliminate the sheet dish from the stove; flip the chicken and broccoli to guarantee in any event, cooking, and equally spoon the vinegar combination over the top.
4. Return dish to the stove and meal for an extra 7 minutes, or until chicken is cooked through and broccoli is fresh delicate. This is an exceptionally blistering stove and on the grounds that all broilers, environment, skillet, and the specific size of the bits of food will shift, so will the specific cooking time.
5. Watch your food and not the clock while deciding whether it's finished. Try not to overcook on the grounds that the chicken will dry out and the broccoli will consume.
6. Optionally trimming with Parmesan and serve right away.
7. Recipe is best new yet will save impermeable in the ice chest for as long as 5 days or in the cooler for as long as 4 months, noticing the

surface of the broccoli will change and get gentler.

6. Old Bay Shrimp and Sausage Sheet Pan Dinner

Serves: 6 | Prep time: 15 min | Cook time: 18 min

Fixings

- 1 lb. Large, crude, shrimp, stripped, deveined, tail on
- 1 chicken hotdog, completely cooked
- 1 lb. Asparagus, managed and cut into 3" pieces
- 2Medium shallots, cut into wedges
- 1 Tbsp. Extra virgin olive oil
- 1 tsps. alt
- 2 tsp. Old straight flavoring
- 1 Lemon
- Pepper, to taste
- Lemon Garlic Aioli
- 1 cup Extra light tasting olive oil
- 1 Egg
- 1 Garlic clove, crushed
- Zest of one lemon
- 1 Tbsp. Fresh lemon juice, from 1 lemon

- 1 tsp. Salt

Technique
1. To make the aioli, add the olive oil, egg, garlic, lemon squeeze and zing and salt to an artisan container. Spot hand blender (otherwise called an inundation blender) at the lower part of the container and turn it on.
2. In a couple of moments you will see the aioli begin to shape at the base. It will rapidly start to emulsify and turn out to be thick.
3. Hold the blender at the lower part of the container for the initial couple of moments until the oil has been fused; at that point move the blender up gradually until completely joined!
4. Heat stove to 400°F.
5. In a huge bowl throw asparagus and shallots in olive oil with 1/2 teaspoon salt and spread on preparing sheet alongside hotdog.
6. Place on focus rack and meal for 10 minutes.
7. Remove skillet from stove and add shrimp. Season whole sheet skillet with staying salt, newly ground pepper, old narrows preparing and press the lemon over the top.
8. Gently throw all fixings on the dish and meal for an extra 6-7 minutes or until hotdog is warmed through and shrimp is pink.
9. Serve warm with the aioli. Appreciate!

7.   Maple Salmon Sheet Pan Dinner

Planning time 10 mins | Cook time 30 mins |
Complete time 40 mins | Serving 2

Fixings

- 1 huge yam cut dainty
- 1 pack asparagus
- 2 pieces new salmon
- Garlic powder to taste
- Salt and pepper to taste
- 2 tablespoons olive oil
- 1-2 tablespoons maple syrup
- Lemon wedges for serving (discretionary)

Directions

1. Preheat stove to 425F, and move the rack to the top third of the broiler. Line a heating sheet with foil for simple tidy up.
2. Using a mandoline, cut the yam into even cuts (I utilized the 4 mm setting). Snap or cut the closures off the asparagus.
3. Place the yam cuts, asparagus, and salmon on the preparing sheet. Coat everything with the garlic powder, salt and pepper, and olive oil.

4. Add the salmon and asparagus to a plate and put away.
5. Spread the yam cuts as uniformly as could really be expected (some cover is alright) on the heating sheet. Prepare for 15 minutes.
6. Add the salmon and the asparagus to the heating sheet (I included the asparagus top of the yam cuts and cleared some space for the salmon).
7. Coat the salmon with a tablespoon of maple syrup. Whenever wanted, shower a second tablespoon of maple syrup across the yams or potentially asparagus too.
8. Bake for an extra 15 minutes, or until salmon is cooked.
9. Serve quickly with some lemon juice crushed over the fish whenever wanted.

8. Sheet Pan Sausage and Potatoes

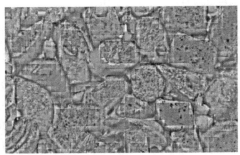

Planning time 5 minutes | Cook time 45 minutes | Complete time 50 minutes | Yield: 5

Fixings

- one 13-ounce precooked hotdog or kielbasa (chicken, pork, turkey, or hamburger frankfurter or kielbasa; I utilized hickory smoked chicken wiener), cut into 1/2-inch adjusts
- 2 pounds Russet potatoes (or your number one potato), diced into 1-inch shapes
- 1 enormous or extra-huge red onion, cut into thick wedges
- 3 to 4 tablespoons olive oil, or more whenever wanted
- 2 teaspoons Italian flavoring, or to taste
- 1 teaspoon genuine salt, or to taste
- 1/2 teaspoon newly ground dark pepper, or to taste
- newly ground Parmesan cheddar, discretionary for embellishing

Directions

1. Preheat stove to 425F (use Convection in the event that you have it). Line a heating sheet with aluminum foil for simpler cleanup whenever wanted.
2. Add the wiener, potatoes, and onions, equally shower with olive oil, equitably preparing with the Italian flavoring, salt, pepper, and throw with your hands to consolidate and cover uniformly.
3. Bake for around 40 to 45 minutes, or until potatoes are delicate and have as much tone as wanted; throw part of the way through preparing to guarantee in any event, cooking.
4. Start checking at 30 minutes for doneness since all stoves, veggies, and so forth change.
5. Optionally sprinkle with Parmesan and serve right away.

9.   Sheet Pan Jambalaya

Planning time 5 minutes | Cook time 15 minutes | All out time 20 minutes | Yield: 6

Fixings

- 12 ounces cooked smoked wiener, cut into slim rounds (Andouille is customary, I utilized smoked hamburger frankfurter)
- 1 medium/enormous yellow onion, cut into flimsy strips
- 4 tablespoons olive oil, isolated
- 3 teaspoons Cajun or Creole flavoring, isolated; or to taste (utilize less for milder flavor)
- 3/4 to 1 pound cleaned and deveined crude shrimp (I incline toward huge 15-20 check shrimp)
- two 8.8-ounce packs cooked rice, warmed by bearings (I favor Spanish-Style Rice) OR 4 cups of your favored cooked rice
- one 16-ounce container thick and stout salsa (I utilized medium warmth)
- 2 to 4 tablespoons green onions, cut into dainty rounds for decorating

Directions

1. Preheat stove to 400F and fix a half sheet skillet with aluminum foil for simpler cleanup. At that point, shower with cooking splash.
2. Add the frankfurter, onions, uniformly shower with 2 tablespoons olive oil, and equitably sprinkle 2 teaspoons preparing.
3. Bake for around 7 to 10 minutes, or until onions relax and wiener 'burns' around the edges.
4. Remove sheet container from the broiler, flip the frankfurter and onions, uniformly add the shrimp, equally shower with the excess 2 tablespoons olive oil, and equitably sprinkle with the leftover 1 teaspoon preparing.
5. Return the skillet to the stove, and prepare for around 4 minutes, or until shrimp are hazy and almost done. In case you're utilizing more modest shrimp, heat for less time (~3 minutes) so they don't overcook.
6. While the sheet skillet is in the stove, to a medium bowl, add the warmed rice, salsa, and mix to consolidate.
7. Remove sheet skillet from the stove, mix and flip the hotdog, onions, and shrimp.
8. Evenly sprinkle the rice and salsa combination, mix to consolidate, and prepare for around 2 minutes, or until everything is warmed through and the shrimp are finished.

9. Evenly enhancement with the green onions and serve right away.

10. Sheet Pan Roasted Sweet Potatoes and Chicken

Planning time 5 minutes | Cook time 30 minutes | All out time 35 minutes | Yield: 4

Fixings

- 2 medium/huge yams, stripped and diced into 1/2-inch pieces
- 3 to 4 tablespoons olive oil, isolated
- 1/2 teaspoon genuine salt, or to taste
- 1/2 teaspoon newly ground dark pepper, or to taste
- 1.25 to 1.50 pounds boneless skinless chicken bosoms, cut into scaled down pieces
- 1 medium/huge red onion, stripped and cut into pieces or wedges
- 1 teaspoon coriander, or to taste

Guidelines

1. Preheat broiler to 425F and fix a preparing sheet with aluminum foil for simpler cleanup.
2. Add the yams, uniformly sprinkle with 2 to 3 tablespoons olive oil, equally season with salt and pepper, throw with your hands to cover

equitably, and heat for 15 minutes. While the potatoes heat, prep the chicken and onion.

3. After 15 minutes, eliminate the heating sheet from the stove, flip the yams, and add the chicken and red onion.

4. Evenly shower with 1 tablespoon olive oil, sprinkle with coriander, and heat for around 15 minutes or until chicken is cooked through and vegetables are delicate.

5. Cooking time will change dependent on the thickness of the chicken, size of potatoes, and being that this is a significant hot stove, check early and regularly so you don't overcook the chicken or consume the potatoes.

6. Serve right away.

11. Sheet Pan Lemon Dijon Baked Salmon and Potatoes

Planning time 5 minutes | Cook time 25 minutes | Complete time 30 minutes | Yield: 4

Fixings

- 2 to 2 1/2 pounds child Yukon Gold potatoes, divided or quartered into 1-inch pieces (infant Red, new potatoes, or another most loved preparing potato might be subbed)
- 5 tablespoons olive oil, separated
- legitimate salt, to taste
- newly ground dark pepper, to taste
- 1/4 cup unsalted margarine, liquefied
- 2 to 3 tablespoons lemon juice
- 2 to 3 tablespoons Dijon mustard
- four 6-ounce skin on salmon filets
- new parsley, finely minced; discretionary for decorating

Guidelines

1. Preheat stove to 425F, alternatively line a heating sheet with rock solid aluminum foil for

simpler cleanup, and shower with cooking splash.

2. Add the potatoes equitably shower with 3 to 4 tablespoons olive oil, uniformly season with salt and pepper, and throw with your hands to join and equally coat.

3. Bake for around 15 minutes, or until potatoes are about 75% done.

4. While the potatoes are preparing, to a little microwave-safe bowl, add the spread and warmth on high ability to dissolve, around 45 seconds.

5. Add the lemon juice, Dijon, and mix to join; put away.

6. Remove the preparing sheet from the stove, flip the potatoes to guarantee in any event, cooking, add the salmon filets skin-side down, uniformly shower with the leftover 2 to 3 tablespoons olive oil, and settle the potatoes around the salmon.

7. Evenly shower around 66% of the lemon spread Dijon combination over the salmon filets. Equally shower the leftover 33% over the potatoes.

8. Some of the combination will overflow the salmon filets; this is ordinary and alright.

9. Evenly season the salmon with salt and pepper, to taste.

10. Bake for around 10 minutes or until the salmon and potatoes are finished.

11. The salmon should chip effectively with a fork and the potatoes ought to be fork delicate.

12. Optionally, for crispier salmon and potatoes, place the sheet skillet under the oven for 2 to

3 minutes, or only until as carmelized as wanted; watch out for your food while it's under the grill since it can consume rapidly.

13. Tip - If you plan on cooking, I suggest diminishing the heating time from 10 minutes to around 7 minutes so neither the salmon nor the potatoes become exaggerated.

14. All thicknesses and cuts of salmon, and potatoes, should cook for marginally various measures of time so watch your food and not the clock and utilize my preparing times just as recommended rules.

15. If your potatoes are done quicker than the salmon, basically eliminate them from the sheet dish and return the sheet skillet back to the broiler until the salmon is finished.

16. Optionally trimming with parsley and serve right away. Formula is best new however will save impenetrable in the ice chest for as long as 5 days.

12. Caramel Apple Sheet Pan Pancakes

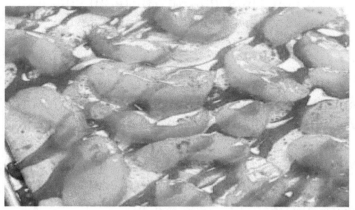

Planning time 5 minutes | Cook time 10 minutes | Absolute time 15 minutes | Yield: one 15x10x1-inch pan

Fixings

- 3 cups Krusteaz Buttermilk Pancake Mix
- 1 teaspoon cinnamon, in addition to additional for sprinkling prior to serving whenever wanted
- 2 1/3 cups water
- one 21-ounce can fruit dessert filling, delicately warmed whenever wanted
- 1/3 cup caramel or salted caramel, or to taste (I utilized natively constructed salted caramel sauce

Guidelines

1. Preheat stove to 400F, line a 15x10x1-inch half-sheet skillet with aluminum foil for simpler cleanup, and shower very well with cooking splash; put away.
2. To a huge bowl, add the hotcake blend and cinnamon, and rush to join.

3. Add the water and rush to join.
4. Turn hitter out into arranged skillet and prepare for around 9 to 10 minutes, or until done; turn container halfway through cooking.
5. Because all broilers, container, and so on shift, begin checking for doneness at around 8 minutes.
6. Evenly top with the apples, sprinkle with extra cinnamon whenever wanted, and uniformly shower with the caramel sauce prior to serving right away.
7. Pancakes are best warm and new however will save impenetrable in the refrigerator for as long as 5 days.

13. Sheet Pan Skinny Lemon Pepper Chicken and Vegetables

Planning time 5 minutes | Cook time 19 minutes | All out time 24 minutes | Yield: 4

Fixings

- Chicken
- around 1 to 1.25 pounds boneless skinless chicken bosoms, cut into reduced down pieces
- 2 tablespoons olive oil
- 2 tablespoons lemon juice
- 2 tablespoons nectar
- 1 teaspoon newly ground lemon pepper preparing mix
- 1 teaspoon legitimate salt, or to taste
- 1/2 teaspoon newly ground dark pepper, or to taste
- Vegetables
- around 3 cups broccoli florets
- 1 medium/enormous yellow or orange ringer pepper, diced into scaled down pieces (another shading pepper might be subbed)

- 1/2 of one enormous red onion, cut into strips or little pieces
- 1 tablespoon olive oil
- 1 to 2 teaspoons newly ground lemon pepper preparing mix, or to taste

Guidelines

1. To an enormous zip top pack, add all fixings, seal sack, and crush everything around to consolidate.
2. Place pack in ice chest to marinate for at any rate 30 minutes and more in the event that you have time. I marinated for the time being.
3. Preheat broiler to 425F, line a heating sheet with aluminum foil for simpler cleanup, and add the broccoli, ringer peppers, and onions, equally shower with olive oil, equitably season with lemon pepper, and throw with your hands to disperse the oil and preparing.
4. Add the chicken to the heating sheet, including additional marinade from the sack, and mix to consolidate it with the vegetables.
5. Bake for around 15 to 19 minutes or until chicken are cooked through and vegetables have some brilliant shading.
6. Toss partially through preparing to guarantee in any event, cooking.

14. Sheet Pan Summer Vegetables and Chicken

Planning time 5 minutes | cook time 20 minutes | absolute time 25 minutes | yield: 4

Fixings

- 1.25 to 1.50 pounds boneless skinless chicken bosoms, cut into reduced down pieces
- 2 medium/enormous zucchini, cut into half-moons or quartered
- 1 medium/enormous yellow squash, cut into half-moons or quartered
- 2 to 3 tablespoons olive oil
- 1 teaspoon newly ground lemon pepper preparing mix
- 1 teaspoon Italian flavoring
- 1/2 teaspoon fit salt, or to taste
- 1/2 teaspoon newly ground dark pepper, or to taste
- 1 medium tomato, diced (I utilized Roma)
- ground Parmesan cheddar, discretionary

Guidelines

1. Preheat broiler to 400F, line a preparing sheet with aluminum foil for simpler cleanup.
2. Add the chicken, zucchini, squash, equitably shower with olive oil, uniformly season with lemon pepper, Italian flavoring, salt, and pepper.
3. Bake for around 17 to 22 minutes or until chicken are cooked through and vegetables are delicate.
4. Cooking time will change dependent on the thickness of the chicken and being that this is a significant hot broiler, check early and regularly so you don't overcook the chicken which can dry out.
5. Add the tomatoes, alternatively decorate with Parmesan, and serve right away.

15. Sheet Pan Orange Ginger Chicken and Vegetables

Planning time 10 minutes | Cook time 15 minutes | Absolute time 25 minutes | Yield: 4

Fixings

- 1 pound boneless skinless chicken bosom, diced into reduced down pieces
- 2 to 3 cups broccoli florets
- 1 cup sugar snap peas
- 1/2 cups carrot cuts (from around 3 medium/huge carrots), cut 1/4-inch thick and on the predisposition
- 1 medium/huge red onion, stripped and cut into reduced down wedges
- 3 to 4 tablespoons olive oil
- 2 tablespoons decreased sodium soy sauce
- 1 to 2 tablespoons stew garlic sauce
- 1 tablespoon fish sauce
- 1 teaspoon orange zing
- 1 to 2 tablespoons squeezed orange
- 2 teaspoons ground ginger
- 1 teaspoon genuine salt, or to taste

- 1 teaspoon newly ground dark pepper, or to taste
- orange cuts, discretionary for decorating
- new cilantro, discretionary for decorating

Directions

1. Preheat stove to 400F and fix a preparing sheet with aluminum foil for simpler cleanup.
2. On one side, add the chicken in a vertical column, close to it add the broccoli in a vertical line, and proceed with every one of the accompanying in vertical lines — the sugar snap peas, carrots, and red onions. T
3. The columns don't need to be awesome, and you can surely dump everything on the sheet skillet in any condition of plan you like; I essentially was going for more accuracy, consistency, and shading hindering.
4. Evenly sprinkle with the olive oil; put away.
5. To a little bowl, add the soy sauce, bean stew garlic sauce, fish sauce, orange zing, squeezed orange, ginger, and rush to join.
6. Evenly brush or spoon the combination over the chicken and vegetables. I thought putting a greater amount of the blend on the chicken instead of the vegetables
7. Evenly season with salt, pepper, and heat for around 15 to 18 minutes, or until chicken is cooked through and the vegetables are fresh delicate.
8. Optionally topping with orange cuts, cilantro, and serve right away.

16. Nectar Citrus Sheet Pan Salmon

Yield: 4 | Time 45 minutes

INGREDIENTS:

- 1 lb. salmon filet, or 4 6oz filets
- Garlicky Potatoes.
- 1 lb. little potatoes, divided
- 2 TBSP olive oil
- 4 cloves of garlic, minced
- 2 TBSP newly cleaved parsley
- A sprinkle of genuine salt and snapped dark pepper
- Asparagus.
- 1-2 lots of asparagus, woody closures severed, See notes.
- 1-2 tsp. olive oil
- A sprinkle of genuine salt and broke dark pepper
- Nectar Citrus Glaze.
- Juice of 1/2 a lime
- Juice of 1/2 a lemon
- Juice of 1/2 an orange
- Juice of 1/2 a grapefruit

- 2 TBSP tamari or low sodium soy sauce
- 1 TBSP nectar
- 1 TBSP coconut palm sugar (or earthy colored sugar)
- 1/2-1 TBSP sambal oelek (or Sriracha)
- 3 cloves of garlic, minced
- 1 tsp. newly ground ginger
- 1 TBSP spread
- 1/4 cup cold water
- 2 TBSP corn starch

Directions

1. Garlicky potatoes.
2. Preheat stove to 400° F. Spot the split potatoes in a huge bowl and shower with olive oil. Throw to cover. Add the garlic, parsley, salt, and pepper.
3. Toss again to cover. Equally circulate the potatoes over a preparing sheet and put bowl away for asparagus. With a spoon, gather up any garlic that has arrived on the skillet and spoon over potatoes. Any garlic set on the dish will consume and welcome on a severe flavor.
4. Bake the potatoes for 20-30 minutes, or until brilliant earthy colored, throwing part of the way through.
5. Nectar Citrus Glaze.
6. Squeeze the lime, lemon, orange, and grapefruit juice into a medium-sized pan. Dispose of any seeds.
7. Add the fixings from the through to the ginger and race until all around joined. Spot the pot over medium warmth and bring to a stew.

8. Simmer until the combination thickens, around 10 minutes.
9. Add the margarine and mix to liquefy. In the event that you'd like a thicker consistency (I generally do), blend the virus water and corn starch into a little bowl, racing with a fork until the corn starch has broken down.
10. Slowly add it to the stewing coat combination, mixing continually until the blend thickens.
11. Remove from warmth and put away.
12. Asparagus.
13. Break off the woody finishes of the asparagus (see notes).
14. Place lances into the bowl your potatoes were in. Sprinkle with olive oil and throw.
15. Sprinkle salt and pepper over the lances, and throw again to cover. Put away.
16. Salmon.
17. Bring the salmon out and set it on the counter 15 minutes before its set to go into the broiler.
18. Bringing the salmon to room temperature will guarantee an even cook. Wipe the salmon off with paper towels and sprinkle with salt.
19. When the potatoes have crisped, free the dish once again from the broiler and set it some place safe. Move the stove rack around 6 crawls from the grill and set oven to high.
20. With a spatula move the potatoes to the sides of the container to make room.
21. Set the salmon down in the center of the container. Appropriate the asparagus around the sides.
22. Carefully pour half of the coating blend over the salmon, brushing it with a seasoning brush

to equitably cover. Put the remainder of the coating away.

23. Cut a couple of slender cuts of the excess citrus foods grown from the ground over the salmon. (Discretionary.)

24. Place the dish under the oven and cook for around 13-15 minutes. Since each grill is extraordinary, watch out for it.

25. It doesn't damage to check the inner temp of the salmon at 8-10 minutes in, and screen it intently after that. You're searching for an interior temperature of 145° F.

26. When done, eliminate the dish from the stove.

27. Carefully dispose of the natural product cuts. Brush the leftover coating over the salmon, cut the filets into 4-6 oz. segments, and serve.

17. Sheet Pan Buddha Bowls with Turmeric Tahini Dressing

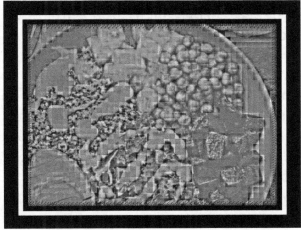

Planning Time: 20 minutes | Cook Time: 20 minutes | All out Time: 35 minutes | Servings: 4 servings

Fixings

- 1 tbsp. olive oil
- 1 medium-sized yam, cut into shapes
- 2 beets, cleaned and cubed
- 1 can chickpeas, flushed and depleted
- 2 tsp. bean stew powder
- 1 tsp. salt
- 1 cup kale, slashed
- 1/2 cup dry quinoa
- 1 cup water
- 1 avocado, cut
- Turmeric Tahini Dressing
- 1/4 cup water
- 2 tbsp. tahini
- 1 tbsp. lemon juice
- 1 tsp. turmeric new or dried

- 1 clove garlic minced
- 1 squeeze salt

Guidelines

1. Preheat broiler to 450 F. On an enormous sheet container, add yams, beets and chickpeas. Throw all fixings with olive oil and season with salt.
2. Rub chickpeas with bean stew powder at that point broil in broiler for 20 minutes.
3. Meanwhile, add quinoa and water to a rice cooker or a pot on the oven and cook.
4. Mix all elements for turmeric tahini dressing together in a food processor, Magic Bullet or blender.
5. Chop kale so it's all set once the dishes are finished cooking.
6. Add all fixings to the dishes, at that point top with tahini turmeric sauce.
7. Serve and appreciate!

18. Sheet Pan Pesto Chicken Meal Prep Bowls

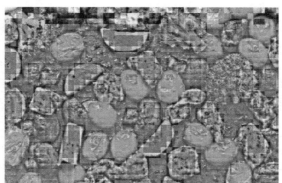

Planning Time: 20 minutes | Cook Time: 20 minutes
| All out Time: 40 minutes | Servings: 4 servings

Fixings

- 2 tbsp. olive oil, isolated
- 1 cup basil, pressed
- 1/4 cup Parmesan cheddar
- 2 cloves garlic minced
- 1/2 tsp. salt
- 1/2 tsp. pepper
- 3 chicken bosoms, diced
- 1 cup mushrooms cut down the middle
- 1 cup Cherry tomatoes
- 1 head broccoli, cut into florets
- 1 little zucchini, cut thickly

Guidelines

1. Preheat broiler to 400 F. In a Magic Bullet, blender or food processor, mix 1 tbsp. olive oil, basil, parmesan cheddar, garlic, salt and pepper together until smooth (you may have to add 1-2 tsp. of water to get it to mix).

2. Add chicken and mushrooms to enormous sheet dish and throw with 1 tbsp. of olive oil and 2 tbsp. of pesto. Heat in stove for 10 minutes.
3. Remove from broiler and channel abundance fluid.
4. Add excess vegetables and the remainder of pesto.
5. Toss to join at that point heat an additional 10 minutes until chicken is completely cooked.
6. Remove from broiler and split between 4 feast prep bowls. Keeps in refrigerator as long as 5 days.

19. Jamaican Chicken Sheet Pan Dinner

Planning Time 15 mins | Cook Time 25 mins | Absolute Time 25 mins | Servings: 4

Fixings

- Jamaican Rub
- 1 tablespoon dried thyme leaves
- 1 tablespoon ground allspice
- 2 tablespoon earthy colored sugar
- 1 teaspoon salt
- 1 teaspoon pepper
- 1 tablespoon garlic powder
- 1 teaspoon cinnamon
- ⅛ teaspoon cayenne for gentle flavor or ¼ teaspoon (for zest ay!)
- Sheet Pan
- 2 huge chicken bosoms
- 4 cups child potatoes cut SMALL in 4-6 relying upon size of potato

- 2 ringer peppers cut into lumps
- 1 red onion cut into lumps
- 1 zucchini cut into little pieces
- To Serve
- 2 mangoes cut into blocks

Guidelines

1. Heat broiler to 425°F. Line two heating sheets with material and put away.
2. Stir together all rub fixings.
3. In a medium measured bowl, throw the chicken with 1 tablespoon of olive oil and 1.5 tablespoons of the rub.
4. Make sure they are equitably covered; at that point organize on one of the preparing sheets.
5. In a different medium measured bowl, throw the potatoes with 1 tablespoon of olive oil and 2 tablespoons of rub.
6. Arrange on the heating sheet around the chicken.
7. Bake for 10 minutes. Flip the chicken and return the container to the broiler for 15 minutes.
8. Toss the peppers, onion and zucchini in 1 tablespoon of olive oil and 2 tablespoons of the rub.
9. Arrange on the subsequent sheet container and prepare for 15 minutes.
10. While sheet container is cooking, set up the mango.
11. Allow the chicken to rest for 5 minutes prior to presenting with the mango.

20. Fresno Chicken Sheet Pan Dinner

Cook Time: 45 mins | Total Time: 45 mins | Yield: 6

Fixings

- FOR THE CHICKEN:
- 6–8 bone-in, skin on chicken thighs or legs (You can utilize skinless in the event that you like)
- 1/2 cup generally useful Fresno bean stew sauce + more sauce for brushing chicken and as a plunging sauce
- FOR THE VEGETABLES:
- 1 yellow chime pepper, cored and cut into enormous strips
- 1 red ringer pepper, cored and cut into enormous strips
- 1 orange ringer pepper, cored and cut into enormous strips
- 2 yams, washed and cut into wedges
- 2 onions, stripped and cut into eights (keep the root on, it keeps the onions flawless)
- 1 1/2 tsp. legitimate salt

- 1 tbsp. olive oil
- 1 tsp. dark pepper
- 1 tsp. thyme

Directions

1. Wash and clean the chicken and wipe off. Throw the chicken in the Fresno stew sauce and let marinate in the cooler for in any event 4 hours.
2. Preheat stove to 450 degrees.
3. Toss the veggies in olive oil, salt, pepper, and thyme. Spread on a sheet container in an even layer.
4. Place bits of chicken on the sheet dish with the veggies.
5. Roast in the stove 40-45 mins, until chicken is totally cooked. In the event that the chicken is consuming, cover freely with a piece of foil.
6. Remove from stove and brush sauce on chicken whenever wanted.

21. Sheet Pan Sausage and Pepper Hoagies

Yields: 4 - 6 servings | Planning time: 0 hours 10 mins | Absolute time: 0 hours 45 mins

Fixings

- 3 chime peppers (red, yellow or potentially orange), cut into huge lumps
- 2 red onions, managed and cut into quarters
- 3 tbsp. olive oil
- 1 tsp. dried sage
- 1 tsp. fit salt
- Black pepper, to taste
- 12 Italian wieners
- 4 hoagie or sub rolls

Headings

1. Preheat the broiler to 425°. Spread the peppers and onions on a heating sheet.
2. Drizzle with the olive oil, sprinkle with the wise, salt and some pepper and throw, separating the onions a piece as you do.
3. Put the hotdogs in and around the vegetables on the preparing sheet.

4. Bake until the hotdogs are cooked through and the vegetables are delicate, 30 to 35 minutes.
5. Slice the hotdogs and serve on moves with the broiled vegetables.

22. Tuscan Pork Sheet-Pan Supper

Yields: 4 - 6 servings | Planning time: 0 hours 35 mins | Absolute time: 1 hour 30 mins

Fixings

- 1/3 c. balsamic vinegar
- 5 garlic cloves, minced
- 1/3 c. furthermore 1/4 cup olive oil, in addition to additional for the skillet
- 4 tsp. dried oregano
- 2 tsp. fit salt, in addition to additional to taste
- 1 1/2 tsp. dark pepper
- 2 pork tenderloins (each somewhat more than 1 pound)
- 6 yams, each cut into 6 wedges
- 6 shallots, quartered
- Chopped new parsley, for fixing

Bearings

1. Whisk the balsamic vinegar, garlic, 1/3 cup olive oil, 2 teaspoons oregano and 1 teaspoon each salt and pepper in a little bowl.

2. Place the pork in a huge resealable plastic sack and pour in the marinade.
3. Seal the pack, place in a dish and marinate for 30 minutes at room temperature or 2 hours in the cooler.
4. Position racks in the upper and lower thirds of the broiler and preheat to 450°. Throw the yams and shallots with the leftover ¼ cup olive oil, 1 teaspoon salt, 2 teaspoons oregano and ½ teaspoon pepper in a huge bowl.
5. Lightly oil 2 sheet containers. Put pork tenderloin on each dish (let a portion of the marinade dribble off first) and season softly with salt.
6. Arrange the yams and shallots cut-sides down around every tenderloin.
7. Roast, turning the skillet partially through and shaking them to extricate the potatoes, until a thermometer embedded into the thickest piece of the meat registers 140° to 145° and the potatoes are delicate, 20 to 30 minutes.
8. Slice the pork and present with the vegetables.
9. Top with parsley.

23. Sheet-Pan Curried Chicken

Yields: 4 - 6 servings | Planning time: 0 hours 15 mins | All out time: 1 hour 0 mins

Fixings

- 1/2 c. red curry glue
- 1 storing tablespoon stuffed dull earthy colored sugar
- 3 tbsp. vegetable oil, in addition to additional for the skillet
- 1 lb. green beans, managed
- 1 lb. carrots, divided longwise and cut into 1/2-inch pieces
- 2 1/2 tsp. genuine salt
- 12 skin-on chicken drumsticks
- 1/3 c. new cilantro, generally cleaved
- Cooked white rice, for serving
- Lime wedges, for serving (discretionary)

Bearings

1. Position a rack in the lower third of the stove and preheat to 425°. Join the curry glue, earthy colored sugar and vegetable oil in a little bowl.

2. Put the green beans and carrots in a huge bowl and throw with somewhat less than half of the curry combination and ½ teaspoon salt.
3. Spread out on an oiled rimmed preparing sheet.
4. Add the chicken and 2 teaspoons salt to the unfilled bowl, add the excess curry combination and throw.
5. Add to the container, nestling the chicken in the vegetables.
6. Roast until the vegetables are delicate and a thermometer embedded into the chicken (without contacting the bone!) registers 170°, 40 to 45 minutes.
7. Turn the vegetables and chicken part of the way through cooking to keep them from getting excessively dull on the base.
8. Scrape the chicken, vegetables and any sautéed bits from the skillet into a huge serving dish and sprinkle with the cilantro.
9. Serve with rice and lime wedges, whenever wanted.

24. Sheet-Pan Cajun Chicken and Corn

Yields: 4 - 6 servings | Planning time: 0 hours 20 mins | All out time: 0 hours 45 mins

Fixings

- 5 tbsp. olive oil, in addition to additional for the skillet
- 6 ears of corn, shucked and cut into 4 pieces
- 5 stems celery, cut on a point
- 2 8-ounce packs child chime peppers, divided and cultivated
- 1 tsp. new thyme
- 4 tsp. Cajun preparing
- 1 tsp. fit salt, in addition to additional to taste
- Black pepper, to taste
- 6 skinless, boneless chicken bosoms (around 8 ounces each)
- 2 garlic cloves, ground
- 2 tbsp. salted spread
- 1/4 c. new parsley, hacked
- Hot sauce, for serving

Bearings

1. Preheat the stove to 425°. Brush 2 rimmed heating sheets with olive oil.
2. Toss the corn, celery and chime peppers with the thyme, 3 tablespoons olive oil, 1 teaspoon every Cajun preparing and salt and a couple of toils of pepper in a huge bowl until very much covered.
3. Divide between the heating sheets and spread in a solitary layer.
4. Add the chicken to a similar bowl. Add the garlic and staying 2 tablespoons olive oil and 1 tablespoon Cajun preparing. Throw well to cover.
5. Add 3 chicken bosoms to each preparing sheet, nestling them in the vegetables. Season with salt and pepper. Heat,
6. pivoting the heating sheets partially through, until the chicken is simply cooked through and the vegetables are delicate, around 25 minutes.
7. Transfer the chicken to a platter.
8. Add 1 tablespoon spread to every plate of vegetables and throw until the margarine softens and the vegetables are coated; add to the platter with the chicken.
9. Top with the parsley and present with hot sauce.

25. Sheet Pan Harissa Chicken With Chickpeas + Eggplant

Planning Time: 10 mins | Cook Time: 40 mins | Absolute Time: 50 mins | Serving 4

Fixings

- 3 tablespoons harissa glue
- 3 tablespoons lime juice from around 2 limes, in addition to more cuts as enhancement
- 2 tablespoons olive oil
- Salt
- 1 15-ounce jar of chickpeas, depleted and flushed
- 1 eggplant diced
- 1/2 red onion stripped and cut
- 1 1/2 pounds chicken I utilized a blend of thighs and drumsticks
- 1 teaspoon minced cilantro as enhancement

Guidelines

1. Preheat broiler to 400 degrees. Line a heating sheet with material paper.
2. In a little bowl, add the harissa glue, lime juice, olive oil and a couple of portions of salt. Speed until joined.

3. To a sheet skillet, add the depleted chickpeas, diced eggplant and red onion.
4. Add portion of the harissa glue combination and combine as one until everything is canvassed in the sauce. Smooth it out into one even layer. Mastermind the chicken on top.
5. Sprinkle the chicken with a couple of portions of salt. Brush the chicken with the harissa sauce and add the any leftover sauce to the chickpeas.
6. Also add any embellishment limes to the sheet dish, on the off chance that you like.
7. Transfer to the broiler to prepare for around 35 to 40 minutes, until the chicken is brilliant earthy colored.
8. Divide among plates and enhancement with some cilantro.

26. Simple Sheet Pan Dinner

Prep Time: 15 minutes | Cook Time: 30 minutes | Yield: 4

Fixings

- 1 crown broccoli (1/2 pound)
- 1 medium red onion
- 1 1/2 pounds yams (around 2 medium enormous)
- 1 pound red potatoes (around 2 medium)
- 1 red pepper
- 1 15-ounce can chickpeas (or 1/2 cups cooked)
- 4 tablespoons olive oil
- 2 teaspoons garlic powder
- 2 teaspoons Old Bay seasoning* (bought or natively constructed)
- 1 tablespoon Italian flavoring
- 1 teaspoon fit salt
- 1 lemon
- Rice or quinoa (or another entire grain or prepared lentils), to serve (discretionary)
- Dollop of acrid cream, Greek yogurt, Vegan Sour Cream, Cashew Cream, or hummus, to serve

Directions

1. Adjust the stove racks for simmering 2 plates. Preheat the stove to 450 degrees Fahrenheit.
2. Chop the broccoli. Cut the onion into thick cuts. Dice the potatoes. Dice the red pepper.
3. Place every one of the vegetables in an enormous bowl.
4. Drain and wash the chickpeas, at that point add them to the bowl. Blend in the olive oil, garlic powder, Old Bay, Italian flavoring, and genuine salt until everything is uniformly covered.
5. Line two preparing sheets with material paper (we favor this to silicone heating mats since it brings about crispier veggies).
6. Spread the vegetables uniformly onto each sheet.
7. Place into the stove and heat for 20 minutes (don't mix!).
8. Remove the container from the stove, pivot them, and meal an additional 10 minutes (for 30 minutes all out) until delicate and daintily seared on one side.
9. Cut the lemon into wedges, and spritz the veggies with new lemon juice to taste. (Required: this progression adds the perfect punch! Or on the other hand you can present with lemon wedges.)
10. Transfer to a serving bowl or dish and serve promptly with rice or quinoa.
11. Dollop with harsh cream, cashew cream or hummus.

27. Quesadillas (Sheet Pan Quesadilla formula)

Planning time 10 mins | Cook time 15 mins | All out time 25 mins | Servings 10 individuals

Fixings

- ½ cup locally acquired salsa See the connection to custom made salsa in note underneath.
- 1 ½ tbsp. custom made taco preparing see notes underneath
- ½ cup plain pureed tomatoes
- 1 lb. ground hamburger
- 3 cup cheddar (I utilized Monterrey jack and Colby blend)
- ⅛ cup diced jolted cooked red peppers
- 10 delicate tortillas
- 2 tbsp. water
- 1 tbsp. flour

Guidelines

1. Preheat broiler to 450°F. Splash a huge 9x13 inch heating sheet with cooking shower.
2. Cover the sheet container in foil or material paper on the off chance that you like, shower the foil/material paper with the cooking splash.
3. In a little bowl add the water and flour and blend well until the bunches have vanished.
4. Set aside.
5. Heat enormous skillet over medium high warmth until hot. Add ground hamburger; cook until carmelized. Channel everything except 2 tablespoons of the fat from the meat. Try not to kill the oven. Add the flavoring blend (see notes), salsa and pureed tomatoes.
6. Add the slurry and blend until the ground hamburger combination thickens. Diminish to stew for 5 minutes. Cool for 10 minutes.
7. Cover the heating sheet with half of the flour tortillas, managing to fit. Sprinkle cheddar and cooled ground hamburger.
8. Place the heating sheet in the broiler a few minutes. Eliminate container from the broiler. Top with the broiled red peppers and more cheddar.
9. Add the remainder of the managed tortillas on top of the cheddar.
10. Bake a few minutes.
11. Open up the broiler and with a wooden spoon or enormous spoon, push down on the quesadillas.
12. Pressing down on the tortillas will straighten them and help them adhere to the cheddar. Eliminate and cut into squares. Enjoy!

28. Sheet Pan Sesame Chicken And Veggies

Prep time 10 mins | Cook time 30 mins | Marinate 30 mins | All out time 1 hr. 10 mins | Servings 4 servings

Fixings

- 2 pounds boneless, skinless chicken thighs or bosoms *pound thicker bosom pieces into even thickness.
- 2 cups broccoli florets
- 1 ringer pepper cultivated and cut into pieces (any tone)
- ½ pound sugar snap peas
- ½ red onion cut into lumps
- Sesame seeds and cut green onions for decorate
- Sauce:
- 1/4 cup oil
- 1/4 cup soy sauce
- 3 tablespoons sesame seeds

- 1 clove garlic minced
- 2 tsp. earthy colored sugar or nectar
- 1 tsp. stew powder
- 1/4 tsp. ground ginger
- 1 teaspoon sesame oil

Guidelines

1. Combine sauce fixings in a little bowl. Put away.
2. Pat chicken dry and spot in a huge zip top sack. Pour marinade over chicken clinched and seal. Back rub the marinade into the chicken to cover.
3. Place in the cooler and marinate for 30-an hour (or overnight).
4. Preheat broiler to 400 degrees F.
5. Arrange veggies on an enormous rimmed preparing sheet and shower two or three tablespoons of olive oil and season with salt and pepper. Throw delicately to cover.
6. Remove chicken from the marinade and organize on the sheet container with the veggies. Dispose of any leftover marinade.
7. Roast in the stove for 20-25 minutes or until veggies are delicate and chicken is cooked through.
8. Broil throughout the previous 5 minutes or so to brown whenever wanted.

29. Magic Sheet Pan Chicken

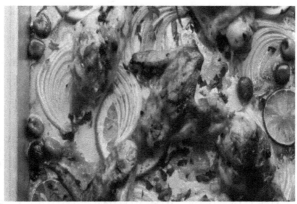

Planning Time: 10 mins | Cook Time: 45 mins | Marinating Time: 3 hrs. | All out Time: 3 hrs. 55 mins | Serving Size 4 individuals

Fixings

- Magic SAUCE:
- 8 cloves of garlic stripped and minced
- 1 teaspoon ocean salt
- 1 tablespoon new or dried oregano
- 1/2 cup olive oil
- 1/4 cup lime juice from around 4 limes
- 1/4 cup squeezed orange from around 1 orange
- 2 pounds bone-in skin-on chicken pieces (I utilized a blend of thighs, drumsticks, wings)
- SHEET PAN:
- 1 yellow onion stripped and cut
- 5 to 6 orange cuts
- 5 to 6 lime cuts
- 1 cup green olives

Guidelines

1. TO MAKE THE MOJO:
2. In a mortar and pestle, add the garlic and salt. Utilizing the pestle, squash and wind the garlic until it's crushed.
3. Add the oregano and give it a decent blend.
4. In a medium bowl or resealable plastic sack (like a Ziploc), add the squashed garlic, olive oil, lime juice and squeezed orange. Utilize a fork to blend it around.
5. Sprinkle the chicken with a couple of portions of salt and pepper and afterward move the chicken pieces to the resealable plastic sack.
6. Seal up the pack and afterward give it a decent shake so the pieces are totally covered in the magic blend.
7. Transfer to the refrigerator to marinate for 3 hours, in a perfect world short-term, however reasonably I realize that will not generally occur.
8. Even marinated for 30 minutes is flavorful! Marinate for anyway long works.
9. At the point when YOU'RE READY TO BAKE THE CHICKEN:
10. Preheat the broiler to 400 degrees F. On a spotless heating sheet, add the onion, cuts or orange and lime, green olives and in conclusion, the marinated chicken, alongside the marinade.
11. Transfer to the stove to prepare until chicken is cooked and skin is firm, around 40 to 45 minutes.
12. Serve with rice, tostones or potentially dark beans. YUM!

30. Garlic-Parmesan Asparagus

Dynamic: 10 mins | All out: 20 mins | Servings: 6

Fixings

- 3 tablespoons extra-virgin olive oil
- 2 cloves garlic, minced
- ½ teaspoon ground pepper
- ¼ teaspoon salt
- 1 ½ pounds new asparagus, managed
- ½ cup finely ground Parmesan cheddar
- 3 tablespoons entire wheat panko breadcrumbs
- 3 tablespoons slashed pecans

Headings

1. Preheat broiler to 425 degrees F. Line an enormous rimmed sheet with foil or material paper.
2. Combine oil, garlic, pepper and salt in an enormous bowl; add asparagus and back rub to equitably cover.

3. Spread the asparagus in an even layer on the readied heating sheet.
4. Toss Parmesan, panko and pecans together in a little bowl; sprinkle over the asparagus.
5. Roast until the panko is brilliant and the asparagus is delicate, 12 to 15 minutes.
6. Serve right away.

31. Broiled Fingerling Potatoes

Dynamic: 5 mins | Complete: 25 mins | Servings: 4

Fixings

- 1 ½ pounds fingerling potatoes, split longwise
- 5 cloves garlic, squashed
- 3 tablespoons extra-virgin olive oil
- ½ teaspoon salt
- ¼ teaspoon ground pepper
- 2 teaspoons hacked new rosemary (Optional)

Bearings

1. Place a rimmed preparing sheet on the center stove rack.
2. Preheat to 450 degrees F.
3. Toss potatoes, garlic, oil, salt and pepper together in a huge bowl.
4. Spread on the hot preparing sheet; broil, mixing part of the way through, until delicate and brilliant earthy colored, around 20 minutes.
5. Sprinkle with rosemary, whenever wanted.
6. Serve right away.

32. Simple Roasted Zucchini and Squash

Dynamic: 10 mins | Complete: 35 mins | Servings: 8

Fixings

- 1 pound medium zucchini, cut corner to corner (1/2-inch)
- 1 pound medium summer squash, cut corner to corner (1/2-inch)
- 3 tablespoons extra-virgin olive oil
- 1 teaspoon salt
- ½ teaspoon ground pepper
- ½ cup approximately stuffed daintily cut new basil
- 2 tablespoons hacked new level leaf parsley

Bearings

1. Preheat stove to 475 degrees F.
2. Toss zucchini, squash, oil, salt and pepper together in a medium bowl.
3. Spread in a solitary layer on a huge rimmed preparing sheet.
4. Roast until mollified and scorched in spots, 20 to 25 minutes.

5. Let cool on the prospect minutes; move to a serving bowl and throw with basil and parsley.
6. Serve hot or at room temperature.

Conclusion

Lastly I hope you liked all recipes in this book .Sheet pan meals are quite easy to prepare and they taste incredible. Try these palatable recipes and enjoy.